The New Novello Choral Edition
NOVELLO HANDEL EDITION

General Editor Donald Burrows

As pants the Hart

(Verse Anthem with organ, HWV 251a)

For soprano, alto, tenor and bass soloists, SATB chorus and organ

Words from Psalm 42

Edited by Donald Burrows

Vocal Score

Order No: NOV290703

NOVELLO PUBLISHING LIMITED

It is requested that on all concert notices and programmes acknowledgement is made to 'The New Novello Choral Edition'.
Es wird gebeten, auf sämtlichen Konzertankündigungen und Programmen 'The New Novello Choral Edition' als Quelle zu erwähnen.
Il est exigé que toutes notices et programmes de concerts, comportent des remerciements à 'The New Novello Choral Edition'.

Permission to reproduce from the Preface of this Edition must be obtained from the Publisher.
Die Erlaubnis, das Vorwort dieser Ausgabe oder Teile desselben zu reproduzieren, muß beim Verlag eingeholt werden.
Le droit de reproduction de ce document à partir de la préface doit être obtenu de l'éditeur.

Published in Great Britain by Novello Publishing Limited
Head Office: 14/15 Berners Street, London W1T 3LJ, UK

Sales and Hire: Music Sales Distribution Centre
Newmarket Road, Bury St Edmunds, Suffolk, IP33 3YB
Tel +44 (0)1284 702600 Fax +44 (0)1284 768301

Web: www.musicsales.com e-mail: music@musicsales.co.uk

 Printed in Great Britain

Music setting by Stave Origination

CONTENTS

PREFACE

This verse anthem was probably Handel's first contribution to English church music and possibly his first setting of an extended English language text. His first dated autograph of an English work, the '*Utrecht' Te Deum*, was completed in January 1713: although *As pants the Hart* is undated and there is no historical record of the anthem's first performance, circumstantial evidence from the appearance of the autograph itself suggests that it probably preceded the Te Deum, and a composition date from November-December 1712 is plausible. After his initial visit to London in 1710-1711, Handel had made a concerted effort to learn the English language, and on his return to England from Hanover in the autumn of 1712 he seems to have been determined to make his mark in those genres that were regarded as particularly 'English': having completed a couple of operas ready for the next season with London's Italian opera company, he turned his attention to the English verse anthem (*As pants the Hart*), the celebratory Anglican canticle (the '*Utrecht' Te Deum and Jubilate*) and the English court ode (*Eternal Source of Light Divine*, for Queen Anne's birthday).

In his choice of words for the anthem, Handel was probably influenced by *Divine Harmony*, a collection of anthem texts published 'with the Approbation of the Sub-Dean of Her Majesty's Chappels Royal' in July 1712. This collection included the words of a version of 'As pants the Hart' attributed to Dr. John Arbuthnot, 'Physician in Ordinary to Her Majesty'. Arbuthnot, who became part of Handel's circle of friends during the composer's first years in London, may have himself composed the anthem represented by the *Divine Harmony* text, or perhaps he selected the words for someone else. (No musical setting survives.) His text comprised a selection of verses from Psalm 42 freely adapted from translations in the Authorised Version of the Bible, the *Book of Common Prayer* and the *New Version of the Psalms* by Tate and Brady. The text that Handel set did not follow that published in *Divine Harmony* exactly, but Arbuthnot's version probably provided him with the starting point for a new selection of verses from the psalm along the same lines.[1]

As pants the Hart seems to have gained a particular place in Handel's affections, for he produced no less than five distinct settings.[2] The present 'verse' anthem with organ accompaniment, composed for the Chapel Royal *c.* 1712-1713, was followed *c.* 1717 by a second setting (HWV 251b) for the chamber group of singers and instrumentalists employed by James Brydges, Earl of Carnarvon and subsequently Duke of Chandos. Some five years later, still Handel composed a revised version of the original verse anthem (HWV 251d), but this was probably never performed. It seems that the special service in the Chapel Royal for which it was intended proved sufficiently significant to qualify for the use of an orchestra, and Handel accordingly recomposed the anthem text again in a new version with orchestral accompaniment (HWV 251c). Finally, Handel took this orchestrally-accompanied anthem as the basis for further expansion, and presented it in a new form (HWV 251e) with his full oratorio forces as the opening item in a benefit performance at the Haymarket Theatre in March 1738.[3] (The two later versions with orchestral accompaniment, HWV 251c and 251e, are available in The Novello Handel Edition.) The musical material of the first two choruses remained fairly constant through all five of the versions (with some re-composition), but the other movements received different treatment and each of Handel's settings has a distinct character. Four distinct types of works are involved: the continuo-accompanied 'verse anthem' (HWV 251a, 251d), the 'chamber anthem' for voices and instruments (HWV 251b), the 'collegiate' Chapel Royal anthem with orchestral accompaniment (HWV 251c) and the 'oratorio' anthem (HWV 251e).

The character of the present version was considerably affected by the musical skills of one of the Chapel Royal's most famous soloists, the alto Richard Elford. (Elford died in 1714, and so his influence was not a factor in Handel's later settings.) William Croft, the Chapel Royal's leading contemporary English composer, described Elford's particular quality as a performer as giving 'a due Energy and proper Emphasis to the Words of his Musick'. After the opening chorus of the anthem Handel gave Elford a complete miniature *scena* consisting of an aria, and arioso and a recitative, the last serving as an introduction to the second chorus. As well as informing himself about the professional strengths of the Chapel Royal choir, Handel had no doubt also taken an interest in the current verse anthem repertory that was performed at the daily services at the Chapel Royal, Westminster Abbey and St. Paul's Cathedral. The ground-bass style of 'Tears are my daily food' (a feature that does not recur in any of Handel's subsequent settings) was perhaps a nod in the direction of the Purcellian tradition, though here (as in other technical aspects of the anthem) Handel's musical treatment may be related to his previous experience in Germany and

Italy as much as to any conscious attempt to follow specific English models. The duet No.4, though entirely appropriate in its anthem context, was recomposed from a movement in Handel's secular Italian duet *Troppo cruda, troppo fiera*, probably composed at Hanover in 1710. Notwithstanding influences and borrowings, Handel's first English verse anthem needs no special pleading with regard to overall design, expressive content, or sensitivity to the English language: it is a lively and well-rounded contribution to the repertory of the English anthem.

Some practical matters

In addition to the principal alto soloist, a soprano or treble soloist is required for the duet (No.4). In the first movement, soloists and chorus alternate: Handel set out the movement for six parts (S/A1/A2/T/B1/B2), but the solo music can easily be taken by four soloists (SATB) as shown in this edition. (The original distribution of the voice parts is indicated and can easily be restored if enough soloists are available.) The Chapel Royal choir, for whom Handel wrote the anthem, was quite small in number and the soloists came from within the 'chorus', so a dramatic distinction between soloists and chorus is not needed: rather, the sections should flow smoothly from one to another. The division of alto and bass chorus voices is only of serious musical consequence in the first movement.

Handel's lightly figured basso continuo accompaniment was clearly intended for organ. In addition to an organist, the Chapel Royal employed a lutenist and a violist. It seems likely that at least the violist (playing either 'cello or viola da gamba) may have accompanied the anthem at its first performance, and in suitable circumstances the addition of such a bass instrument would be appropriate in modern performances.[4] The presence of an independent bass instrument at the Chapel Royal may explain the apparently forbidding layout of Handel's accompaniment in No.2 bars 56-72, where the simultaneous accommodation of Handel's obbligato part,[5] his bass line and some continuo 'filling' may prove impossible for players with small hands. Several practical solutions are possible. The bass line may be entrusted to a stringed instrument or to the organ pedals (possibly coupled to the accompanying manual and with no independent pedal stops). On some organs, depending on the voicing of the stops, Handel's obbligato and bass lines may make musical sense alone, with little or no filling out of inner parts: otherwise, the manuals-only accompanist will have to resort to such compromises as are practical. On some organs it will be possible to distinguish obbligato and accompaniment by the use of two manuals.

The organ in the Chapel Royal, St. James's Palace, had been built by Bernard Smith only a few years before Handel composed the anthem. This instrument has long since vanished, but a reasonable reconstruction of its specification can be made from an early nineteenth century source:

Great	Chaire
Open Diapason	Stopped Diapason
Stopped Diapason	Principal
Principal	Flute
Twelfth	Cremona
Fifteenth	
Sesquialtera III	
Trumpet	

The pitch of the organ was probably sharp, even by modern pitch standards. Limitations of space within the organ gallery restricted the compass to CC-c‴ (or possibly CC-d‴), and the trumpet was apparently a short-register stop. The chair organ was within the main case. The Chapel was quite small, and allowance must be made for the relatively sweet and light tone of English organs of the period. Much of the anthem was probably accompanied by 'soft' combinations of stops such as Great Diapasons (Open and Stopped Diapasons together) or Great Diapasons and Principal, rising to something like full organ (probably without Trumpet) in the central and final chorus movements. A bright registration would be suitable for the duet and for No.2 bars 73-84, at a volume level appropriate to balance the voices. In the chorus movements the continuo realisation does not double the soprano in the upper register, but eighteenth century English practice in this matter is uncertain. In many places it would be easy to incorporate the soprano part into the right hand if circumstances require it.

Sources

Primary Source

A British Library Additional MS 30308, ff. 17-26. Handel's composition autograph of the complete anthem. Watermark E*10, of a type unique in Handel's autographs.[6] 16-stave paper, ruled with 2-stave rastra with span 30.5 mm, identical to that found in a section of Handel's autograph of the opera *Rinaldo*, 1711 (Cambridge, Fitzwilliam Museum, MU MS 254, pp.45-6, 49-54).

In the autograph Handel named the following singers, all from the Chapel Royal:[7]

No.1 Mr. [Francis] Hughs (Alto 1);
Mr. Eilfurt [i.e. Elford] (Alto 2);
Mr. [Samuel] Whely [Weely] (Bass 1);
Mr. [Bernard] Gates (Bass 2)

No.2 Mr. Eilfurt (three times)

No.4 The Boy; Mr. Eilfurt

No.5 Initials and names as No.1

At the first vocal entries of Nos.4 and 6 Handel wrote 'Chorus partout'. Handel gave no instrumental specification for the basso continuo staves or for the obbligato part in No.2.

B British Library RM 20.g.10 ff. 23-26. Handel's autograph of his second verse anthem setting of *As Pants the Hart* (HWV 251d), *c.*1722. Watermark B50; 10-stave paper ruled with 2-stave rastra, span 30 mm. This anthem includes movements reworking music from Nos.1, 3 and 5 of the present setting.

C British Library RM 19.g.1 vol.1 ff. 30-39. Manuscript full score, in the hand of copyist S11, *c.* 1765. Watermark type F; 10-stave paper ruled with 10-stave rastra with span c. 197 mm. The volume is from the so-called 'Smith Collection',[8] and was part of the Royal Library by 1772. This copy was probably the source-text for the first printed edition, Händel-Gesellschaft vol. 34 (Leipzig, 1871, ed. F. Chrysander) pp. 277-288 ('Anthem VIc').

D Rutgers University Library, New Brunswick, U.S.A. M2038.H14A5, Vol.IX pp. 99-126. Manuscript full score, in the hand of 'Copyist A',[9] *c.*1765, derived from copy **C**, in a volume from the collection formed by Sir Watkins Williams Wynn (4th baronet, d.1789). An entry in the contents page to the volume, possibly in the hand of copyist S10, reads: 'As pants the Hart &c Adapted for voices without instruments, for the Chapple Royal, by command of the late King'. This information is clearly erroneous: HWV 251a must, on the evidence of Elford's name among the singers, precede Handel's versions of *As pants the Hart* with instrumental accompaniment. The confusion may have arisen because William Boyce later produced a verse anthem based on Handel's 'Chandos' version of *As pants the Hart*, probably in the last years of George II's reign.[10]

E Bodleian Library, Oxford, MS Mus. d. 57, pp. 149-174. Manuscript full score, *c.* 1765, in the hands of three scribes including Philip Hayes, and derived from copy **D**. It occurs in volume 8 from a series of anthem manuscripts originating from Oxford musicians, and possibly first owned by William or Philip Hayes, successively Heather Professors of Music at the University of Oxford. The title on p.149 reads: 'As Pants the Hart (as perform'd at the King's Chapel, in the reign of George the 2d at whose command it was put into its present state from the original) '; this was added by Philip Hayes, presumably from the information in the index to copy **D**.

Occasional comparative reference has also been made to the primary sources for Handel's other versions of the anthem, HWV 251b (British Library RM 20.d.6) and HWV 251c (British Library RM 20.g.1 and Add. MS 31557). In addition to Chrysander's edition, already noted, the anthem has been published in *Hallische Händel-Ausgabe* Serie III Band 9, ed. Gerald Hendrie (Kassell, 1992); the editorial work for the present edition had been completed before this appeared.

Editorial Procedure

This edition is based on Source **A**, with only a limited contribution from the secondary sources. Source **B** has been used for clarification on some points of detail in the choruses based on the same music. Copies **D** and **E** have no textual authority independent of Copy **C**, and comparison with the autograph reveals that the text of **C** (which may well be derived from a lost intermediate copy) includes, as well as some dubious musical readings, the results of some editorial emendation of Handel's word-underlay according to conventions that were thought to be more appropriate to the treatment of the English language later in the eighteenth century. The verbal text of this edition has been prepared on the basis of what contemporary scribes and performers could reasonably have produced from Source **A**.

Clefs, rhythmic note-grouping and accidentals have been modernised. Handel wrote for treble (Canto), alto and tenor voices in the appropriate C clefs. His system for accidentals generally leaves no doubt about his intentions, and the few clarifying editorial interventions are shown in small type; editorial additions to tempo markings and the like are shown in square brackets. Editorial ties are shown thus: ⌒, and hemiola re-groupings at triple-time cadences are signalled editorially by square brackets above and below the system. Handel indicated the textual underlay with the minimum number of verbal cues: these have been interpreted editorially, and any points of ambiguity are recorded in the commentary. Figuring is reproduced from Source **A** and, in No.1, from Source **B**: apparently 'inverted' figure-groups have been modernised. Editorial continuo realisation of the bass line is shown in smaller music-type. The division into movements is editorial, though clearly implied by the music. The autograph contains ten slurs in the vocal parts: nine of them merely clarify the rhythm of the text-underlay and the remaining one (No.2 bar 81, first two notes of beat 4) probably relates to an idea for word-underlay that was not finally carried through. The slurs have been omitted, as having no further implications for phrasing.

Commentary

No.1

The distribution of music for SATB soloists in this movement is editorial: the original voices (S A1, A2, T, B1, B2) are indicated above the voice entries so that the original arrangement may be restored if 6 soloists are available. 'Solo' vocal indications in this movement that are clearly implied by the singers' names in the autograph at the opening have been included without editorial brackets.

Handel misspelt 'pants' as 'paints' throughout the movement. In **A** handel figured the continuo only at bar 28 (beats 1, 3), bar 40 (beats 1-2 figured '2, ♭'), bar 44 (beat 3) and bars 52-3: all other figurings are reproduced from **B**. These have not been followed slavishly in the realization.

bar

1 Tempo indication from **B**. Handel's orchestrally-accompanied versions have 'Adagio' (HWV 251b) and 'Largo' (HWV 251c).

1-2 Bc. Handel made two attempts at the opening before settling on the final version:

4 Bc. Figuring beat 3 from **B** omitted (different bass note).

16 A2. Handel first wrote 'tutti', before replacing the word with 'chorus'.

20-27 A1, A2. No word-underlay; T has none bars 21-27. The editorial solution is based on **B**. At bar 21 A1 and A2 are identical to the end of the bar in **A**: A1 from **B** adopted.

27 *et seq* Several slurs were added by Handel here to clarify the syncopated rhythm of the word-underlay.

28 Bc. 4 figuring in **A**, 4+ in **B**.

35,39 Bc. Figuring '9' on beat 1 in **B**, apparently not appropriate to this version.

36-8 A1. Handel made two layers of alterations to these bars: his final decision is clear, but he forgot to delete music in bar 37, which at one stage doubled A2.

44,50 Chorus cues have 'so longs my soul to Thee' (c.f. 'for Thee' at previous occurrences).

51-55 This passage was recomposed in **B**, so irrelevant figurings from this source have been omitted.

51-52 Bc. Altered by Handel from:

No.2

bar

1 Tempo indication derived from Handel's at bar 25.

19,46,81 Slurs added by Handel in these bars to clarify underlay.

20 **A** has dotted minim.

32-33 Handel spread 'a-re' as if two syllables, though he treats the word as one syllable elsewhere.

37 'they' altered by Handel from 'Thy'

45,50,84 Handel did not add clarifying slurs to the underlay at these places, but the most likely solutions implied by his word-spacing have been adopted editorially.

55 et seq Single bar-lines at the end of bars 55, 72, but double bar after 60. The order of staves at bars 56-50 is voice/(organ)/bc, but at bars 61-72 (organ)/voice/bc.

57 (Organ). Last 3 notes : beam omitted.

59 Bc. Semibreve

60 Bc. Last note minim

71 Bc. Second note altered by Handel from c′.

72-3 Single barline

76 Handel's notation is clear here, though the mid-bar hiatus is unusual and the omission of 'for' was presumably intentional.

79 Bc. Last note minim

84 Originally followed by an instrumental postlude thus:

	Handel deleted this and added the cue 'segue chorus'.

No.3
bar

1	Tempo direction from **B**. HWV 251c also has 'allegro'.
1 *et seq*	Voices. Comma after 'praise' added editorially.
1,3	'Chorus par tout'/'Chorus' added by Handel in pencil over the vocal entries.
9	T. Handel wrote 'and thanksgiving' (c.f. 'of thanksgiving' at every other occurrence).

No.4
bar

1	Editorial tempo indication derived from the musically-related movement in the Italian Duet HWV 198; no autograph for the duet survives, but copies have 'andante'.
14-15	S; also 23-24 A, 31-32 S&A, 44-46 S&A, 56-57 S, 62-63 S&A, 69-70 S&A. Handel's word-setting of 'Why [so] disquieted within me' is inconsistent: compare, for example, the stress patterns at bars 62-3 and 69-70. The intentions that can be discerned from the autograph have been followed, though they are unclear in a few places. At bars 31-32 the reading of the autograph is clear but the voices seem badly synchronised and an alternative editorial amendment has been suggested. In general Handel seems to have regarded 'disquieted' as 3 syllables: see bars 24, 38 and 42 S, and bars 37, 39 and 57 A. It is just possible that Handel intended the word-arrangement of bars 61-63 to prevail elsewhere, and that the 4-syllable treatment is the result of careless orthography.

No.5
Handel laid out 'prai-se' in several instances as if it had two syllables: examples include '-se' at bar 6 beat 2 A,T, bar 14 beat 2 S. However, the bass voice in these bars shows that the word is to be treated as one syllable.
bar

1	Tempo indication from **B**: there is none in **A**. There is no parallel movement in other versions of the anthem.
1,3	Handel wrote 'Chorus'/Chorus partout' in pencil over the first vocal entries.
3-6	Handel laid out the movement with two alto parts, labelled originally for Hughs and Elford, though these designations were presumably effectively cancelled by 'Chorus partout' over A1 at bar 3. From bar 6 beat 2 A2 is identical to A1, but the opening entry of A2 doubles T: this distinction, which seems to reflect 'solo' thinking that was superseded by subsequent 'choral' treatment, has been suppressed.
16	S. Word-underlay 'prai-se for' ('him' omitted by Handel).
16	B. Word-underlay clarified by slur in B2 (autograph has identical B1, B2 music throughout movement).
19-22	Various compositional alterations to the vocal parts, but the final readings are clear.
20-21	The consecutives between T and B were repeated by Handel 10 years later in **B**.
24	A. Beat 3. Handel wrote quavers c″, a′ (on both A1 and A2 staves), giving consecutive octaves with **B**. Revised editorially from **B**.
39-40	Various compositional alterations to the vocal parts, but the final readings are clear.
43-44	Corner of autograph lost, taking music for T, B and Bc. Text restored from **C**. (No parallel passage in **B** or any other versions of the anthem).

Acknowledgements
I thank the owners and keepers of the relevant library collections for access to the sources for the anthem. The edition is based on one initially prepared for a performance by the Abingdon and District Musical Society with Ashley Stafford (Alto), and conducted by the editor.

1 For the detailed history of Handel's anthem see Donald Burrows: *Handel and the Chapel Royal during the Reigns of Queen Anne and King George I* (dissertation, Open University, 1981), Vol. 1 Chapter 3; also Graydon Beeks: 'A Club of Composers' in Stanley Sadie and Anthony Hicks (eds.): *Handel Tercentenary Collection* (London 1987) pp.215-217.

2 See Donald Burrows: 'Handel's "As Pants the Hart"', *The Musical Times*, Vol. cxxvi (1985), pp.113-6.

3 See Donald Burrows, 'Handel's 1738 "Oratorio": A Benefit Pasticcio' in Klaus Hortschansky and Konstanze Musketa (eds.), *Georg Friedrich Händel - ein Lebensinhalt* (Halle an der Saale, 1995), pp.11-38.

4 The continuo bass part from this edition may be copied from this score for use in performances.

5 In the first published edition of this anthem (1871), Friedrich Chrysander assigned this obbligato part provisionally to solo oboe or violin. The introduction of a new instrument for these few bars alone is inherently implausible, and the layout of the staves in Handel's autograph strongly implies that the obbligato is a 'right-hand' part for organ.

6 For watermark designations, see Donald Burrows and

Martha J. Ronish, *A Catalogue of Handel's Musical Autographs* (London, 1994) and (for watermarks and copyists) Jens Peter Larsen, *Handel's "Messiah": Origins, Composition, Sources* (London, 1957).

7 Spellings are transcribed literally, and minor losses from names at the margin have been made good in the list.

8 See Donald Burrows, 'The "Granville" and "Smith" Collections of Handel Manuscripts', in Chris Banks, Arthur Searle and Malcolm Turner (eds.), *Sundry sorts of music books* (London, 1993), pp.231-247.

9 See Martin Picker: 'Handeliana in the Rutgers University Library', *Journal of the Rutgers University Library*, vol. xxix No.1 (1965), p.1.

10 See Graydon Beeks, 'William Boyce's adaptations of Handel's works for use in the English Chapel Royal', *Händel-Jahrbuch* 39. Jahrgang (1993), pp.42-59.

AS PANTS THE HART

No. 1 — Soloists and Chorus AS PANTS THE HART FOR COOLING STREAMS

Psalm xlii, 1

Chorus with S.A.T.B. soli

A tempo ordinario

ALTO SOLO *[A2]

As pants the Hart for

A tempo ordinario

Continuo (Organ + 'cello or viola da gamba, *ad libitum*)

[*mf*]

[Verse]

SOPRANO SOLO[S]

As pants the Hart for cool - - ing

cool - - ing streams, for___ cool - - - - - - ing

streams, for___ cool - - - - - - ing streams,

streams, for___ cool - - - ing, cool - ing streams,

TENOR SOLO [B1]

As pants the Hart for

BASS SOLO [B2]

As pants the

*Handel's score distributes the solos in this movement among six soloists (SAATBB): see Preface and Critical Commentary. The original voices are shown in brackets at each entry.

10

As pants the Hart for cool -

[A1]

As pants the Hart for cool - ing streams, for

cool - ing, cool - ing streams, for cool - - - - - - ing

Hart for cool - ing streams, As pants the

10

7 3 4 4 # 7 6
2

13

- ing streams, for___ cool - - - - - - - - -

cool - - - ing streams, for cool - - -

streams,

Hart for cool - - - - - - - - ing streams, for

13

7 # 2 6 7 6 7 7
5

16
[with chorus]
- ing streams, as pants the
[with chorus]
- ing streams, for cool - - ing streams,
[with chorus]
for cool - - ing streams, for cool - -
cool - ing streams,
16
Chorus
SOPRANO
As pants the
ALTO
As pants the Hart for cool - - ing streams,
TENOR
As pants the Hart for cool - -
BASS
[più f]
16
5♮ 4 # 6 5 4 4 # 7 6 7 #
19
Hart for cool - ing streams, as pants the Hart for cool -
cool - ing streams,
div.
for cool - ing streams, for cool - - - -
- - - - ing, cool - - - - - - - - - -
As pants the Hart for cool - ing streams, for
16
4 # 7 6 6 # 4 2 4 2 6
[Chorus]

22

- ing streams, as pants the Hart for cool - -

for cool - - - - - - - unis. - - - - - -

- ing, cool - - - - - - - - - - - - -

- ing streams, for cool - - - - - - - - - - -

div. 1

2

cool - ing streams, for cool - - - - - - - -

22

7 6 ♮ 5 6 4 5 4 ♭3 7 6 4 5 4 6 5

25

- - - ing streams, for cool - ing, cool - ing streams,

- - - ing

div.

- - - ing streams, for cool - ing, cool - ing streams,

- - - ing streams, for cool - ing, cool - ing streams,

unis. div.

- - - ing streams, for cool - ing, cool - ing streams,

25

6 5 6 5 6 5 9 6 ♮ 7 4 ♯

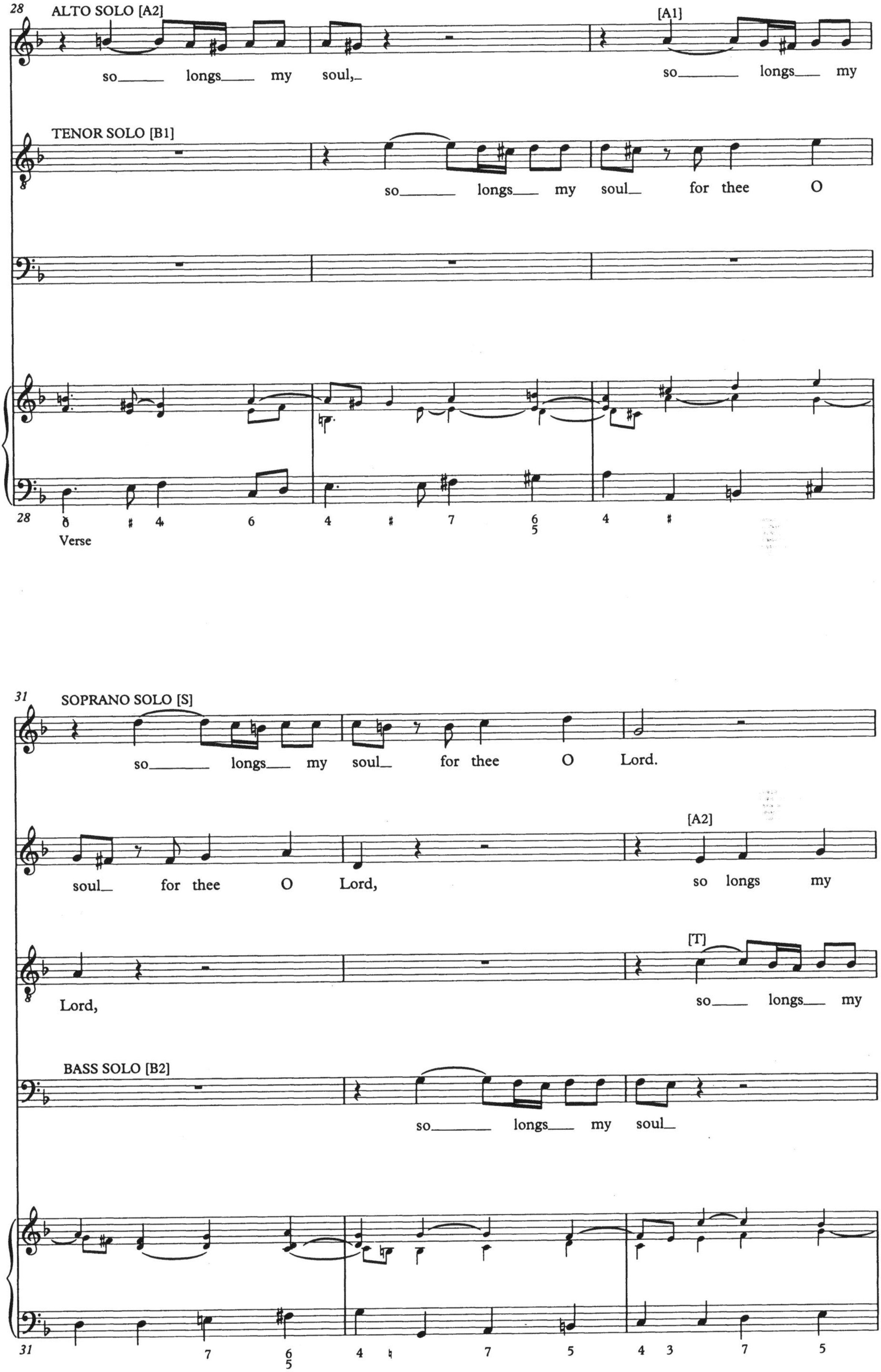

31 SOPRANO SOLO [S]

so___ longs___ my soul_ for thee O Lord.

soul_ for thee O Lord,

[A2]

so longs my

Lord,

[T]

so___ longs___ my

BASS SOLO [B2]

so___ longs___ my soul_

31

34
[with chorus]
As pants the Hart for cool - - ing
soul for thee O Lord.
[with chorus]
As
soul for thee O Lord.
[with chorus]
So
[with chorus]
So longs my soul for thee O
Chorus
SOPRANO
As pants the Hart for cool - - ing
ALTO
so long my soul for cool - ing streams
As
TENOR
So
BASS
so longs my soul for thee O
[più f]
[Chorus]
37
streams, so longs my soul, so longs my
As pants the Hart for
pants the Hart for cool - - - ing streams,
longs my soul for thee O Lord, so longs,
Lord. As pants the Hart for cool - - - -

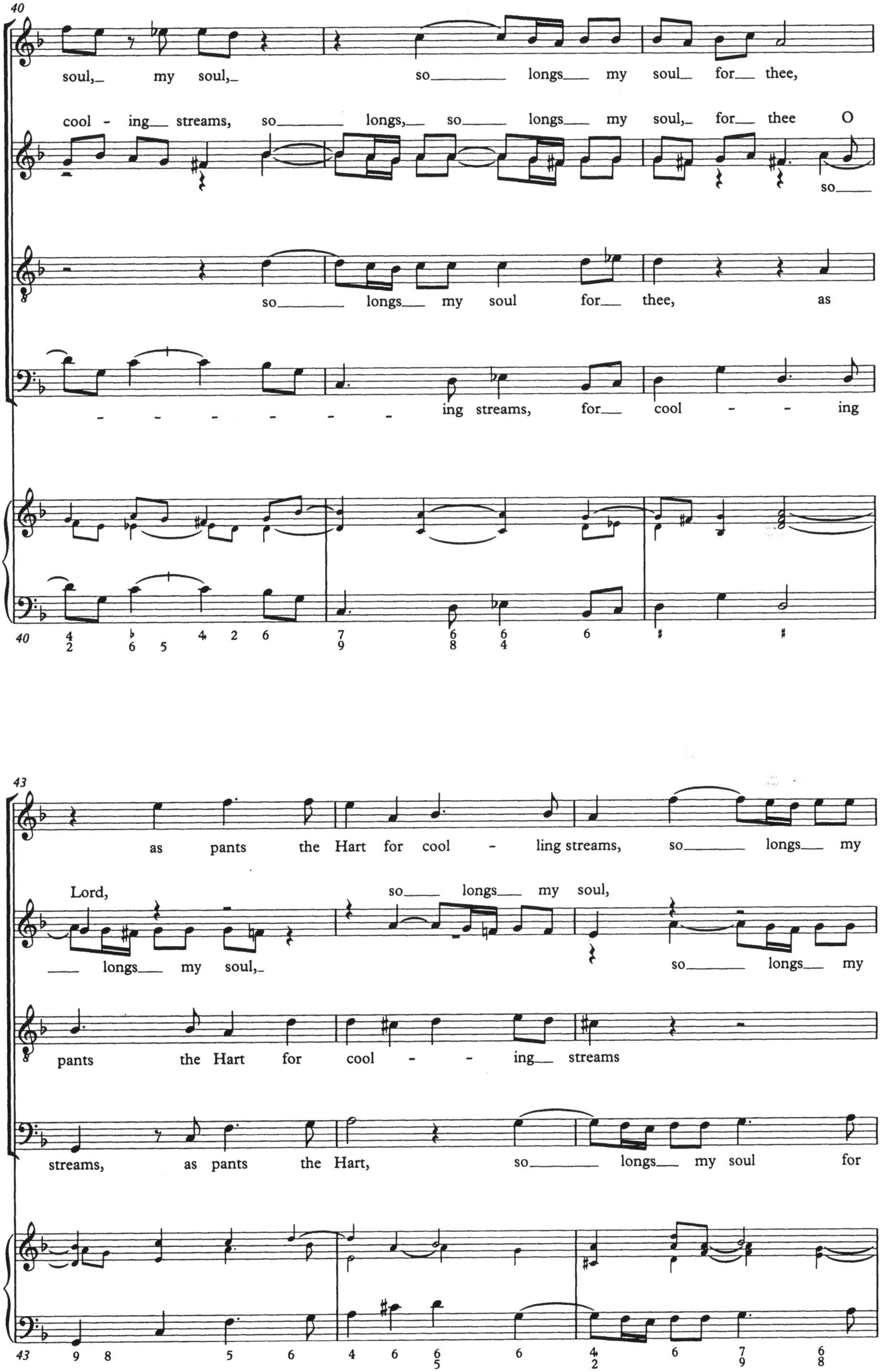

40

soul, my soul, so longs my soul for thee,

cool - ing streams, so longs, so longs my soul, for thee O

so

so longs my soul for thee, as

- - - - - - ing streams, for cool - - ing

40

46
soul, so longs my soul,
so longs my soul, so longs my soul,
soul, so longs my soul, so longs my soul,
so longs my soul, so longs my soul,
thee, so longs my soul,
46
49
so longs, so longs my soul for thee, O Lord.
so longs, so longs my soul for thee, O Lord.
so longs, so longs my soul for thee, O Lord.
div.
so longs, so longs my soul for thee, O Lord.
49
52

No. 2 Air and Recitative TEARS ARE MY DAILY FOOD

Psalm xlii, 3-4

Alto Solo

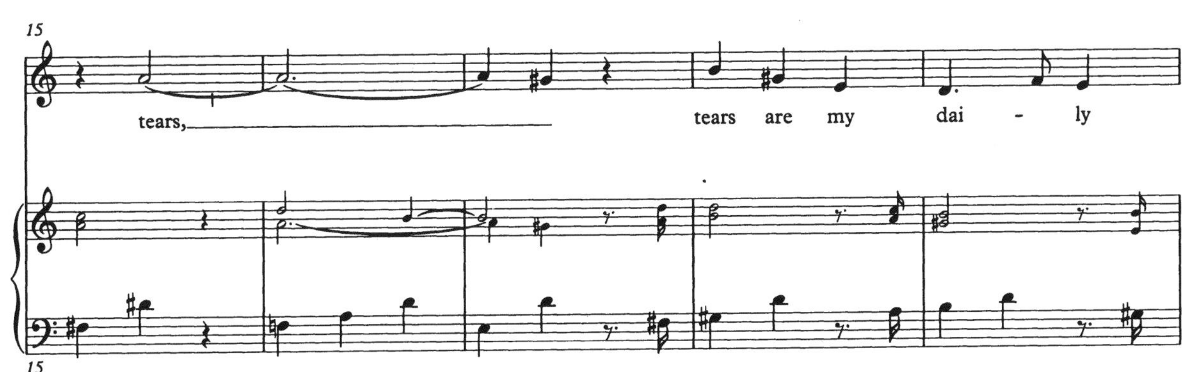

Adagio
food, are my dai - ly food,
Adagio
Andante
tears, tears are my
Andante
[p]
dai - - - - - ly food, are my dai -
[tr]
- - ly food, when thus they say, when thus they
[tr]
* Ornamentation of the solo part would be appropriate here, e. g.
tr

* See Preface concerning the performance of the organ part in this section.

60
Now when I think there - u - pon,
60
64
now when I think there - u - pon I pour out my heart by my-
64
68
- self, I pour out my heart by my - self.
68
73 [Recit, più mosso]
For I went with the mul - ti - tude and brought them out in - to the House of God, I
[Recit, più mosso]
[f]
73

No. 3 Chorus IN THE VOICE OF PRAISE, OF THANKSGIVING

Psalm xlii, 5

Chorus

In the voice of
a - mong such as keep ho - ly, ho - ly - day,
Praise, of thanks - gi - ving a - mong such as keep ho - ly, ho - ly - day.
ho - ly - day. a - mong such as keep ho - ly - day, a - mong such
Praise, of thanks - gi - ving a - mong such as keep ho - ly -
In the voice of Praise, of thanks - gi - ving a - mong such
In the voice of Praise, of thanks - gi - ving
as keep ho - ly, ho - ly - day.

9
-day, as keep ho - ly - day,
as keep ho - ly - day, as keep ho - ly - day. In the voice of
of thanks - gi - ving a - mong such as keep ho - ly - day, keep
In the voice of Praise, of thanks - gi - ving a - mong such
9

12
a - mong such as keep ho - ly - day, a - mong such as keep ho -
Praise, of thanks - gi - ving a - mong such as keep ho - ly - day, a - mong such as keep
ho - ly - day, a - mong such
as keep ho - ly - day, a - mong such as keep ho - ly - day,
12

15
- ly - day. In the voice of Praise, of thanks-gi - ving a-mong such
ho - ly-day, as keep ho-ly - day, a-mong such as keep
as keep ho-ly - day, a-mong such as keep ho - ly-day, a-mong such as keep
a-mong such as keep ho-ly-day, a-mong such as keep ho-ly-
15

18
as keep ho-ly-day, a-mong such as keep ho-ly-day, a-mong such as keep ho -
ho-ly, ho-ly-day, a-mong such as keep ho-ly-day, keep ho - - - ly -
ho-ly-day, a-mong such as keep ho-ly-day, a-mong such as keep ho-ly, ho-ly -
-day, a-mong such as keep ho-ly-day, a-mong such as keep ho - ly-day,
18

21
- ly - day.
-day, a - mong such as keep ho - ly - day, a - mong such
-day, a - mong such as keep ho - ly -
In the voice of Praise, of thanks - gi - ving a - mong such as keep ho - ly - day.
21

24
In the voice of Praise, of thanks - gi - ving a - mong such as keep ho - ly-day, a -
as keep ho - ly - day, as keep ho - ly - day, a -
- day, In the voice of Praise, of thanks - gi - ving a - mong such
In the voice of Praise, of thanks - gi - ving a - mong such as keep ho - ly -
24

No. 4 Duet WHY SO FULL OF GRIEF, O MY SOUL?

Psalm xlii, 14

S. A. soli

[Andante]

[*mf*]

5

SOPRANO SOLO

Why, why, why so

5

10

full of grief O my soul, why dis - qui - et - ed

10

15
with - in
me? Why so
full of grief
ALTO SOLO
Why,
why,
why so
19
O my soul,
O my soul,
why dis -
full of grief
O my soul, why dis - qui - et - ed
24
-quiet - ed with - in me?
Why,
why
so full of
with - in
me?

* Editorial alternative: see Commentary.

Soprano: bars 55-8 underlay unclear; possibly also why dis - quiet - ed with - in me in soprano part instead.

58
me? Why,___ why,___ why so dis - quiet - ed with -
me? Why,___ why,___ why so dis - quiet - ed with -
58
63
- in me? Why? Why?
- in me? Why? Why?
63
68
Why dis - qui - et - ed___ with - in me?
Why dis - qui - et - ed___ with - in me?
68
73

No. 5
Psalm xlii, 15

Chorus PUT THY TRUST IN GOD

Chorus

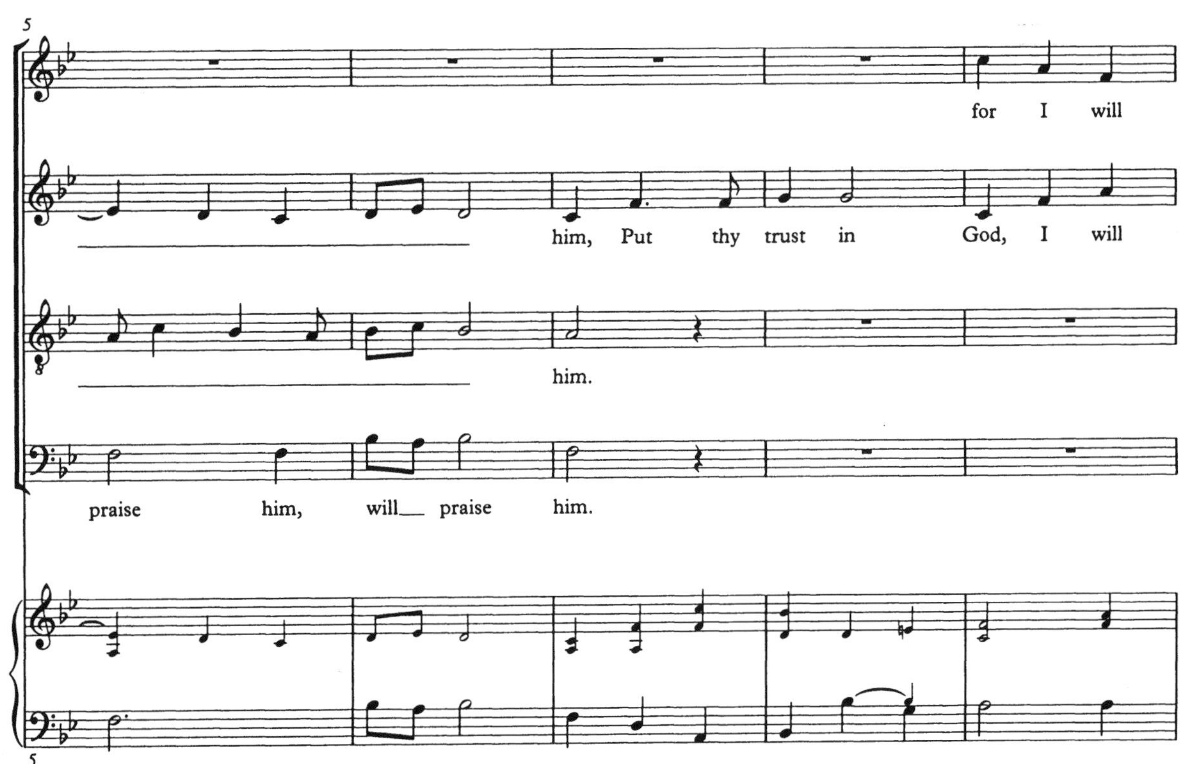

* In Handel's autograph an Alto 2 soloist doubles the tenor part up to bar 6 beat 2, following the Alto chorus part thereafter.

10

praise___

praise___

for I will praise for I will

for I will praise him,___

him,

10

14

___ him, I will praise him, for___ I will praise him

___ him, Put thy trust in

praise___ him.

___ will praise him, for I___ will praise___

14

* The consecutives between Tenor and Bass are clear in Handel's autograph. The small notes are an editorial alternative.

27

praise him, for I will praise him, wil praise

27

31

Put thy trust in God, I will praise

him, I will praise him,

him, for I will praise

him, for I will

31

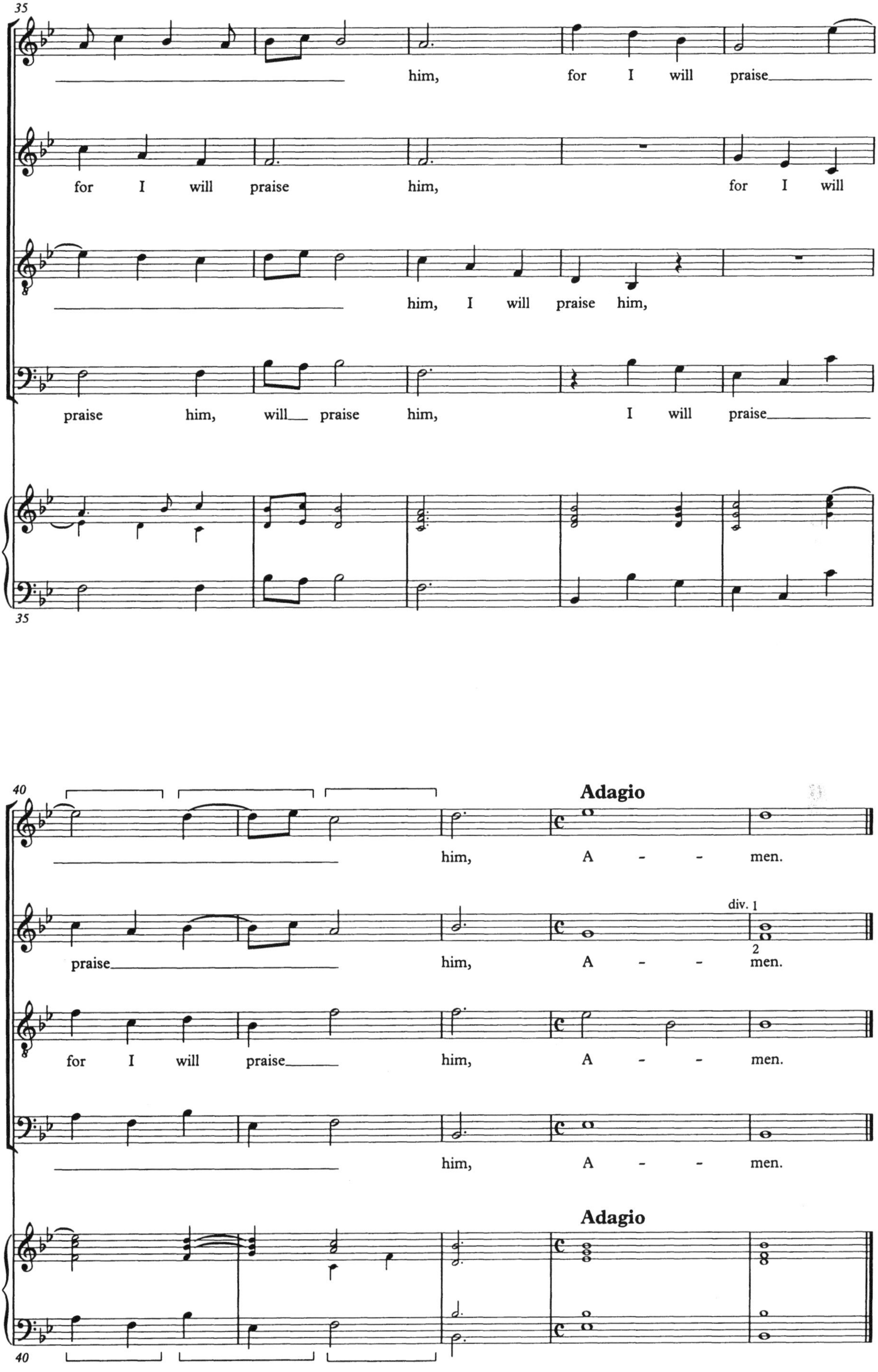

35

him, for I will praise

for I will praise him, for I will

him, I will praise him,

praise him, will praise him, I will praise

35

Printed and bound in Great Britain by Caligraving Limited